The Little Church

A Tale About Bats, Churches And The People Wh

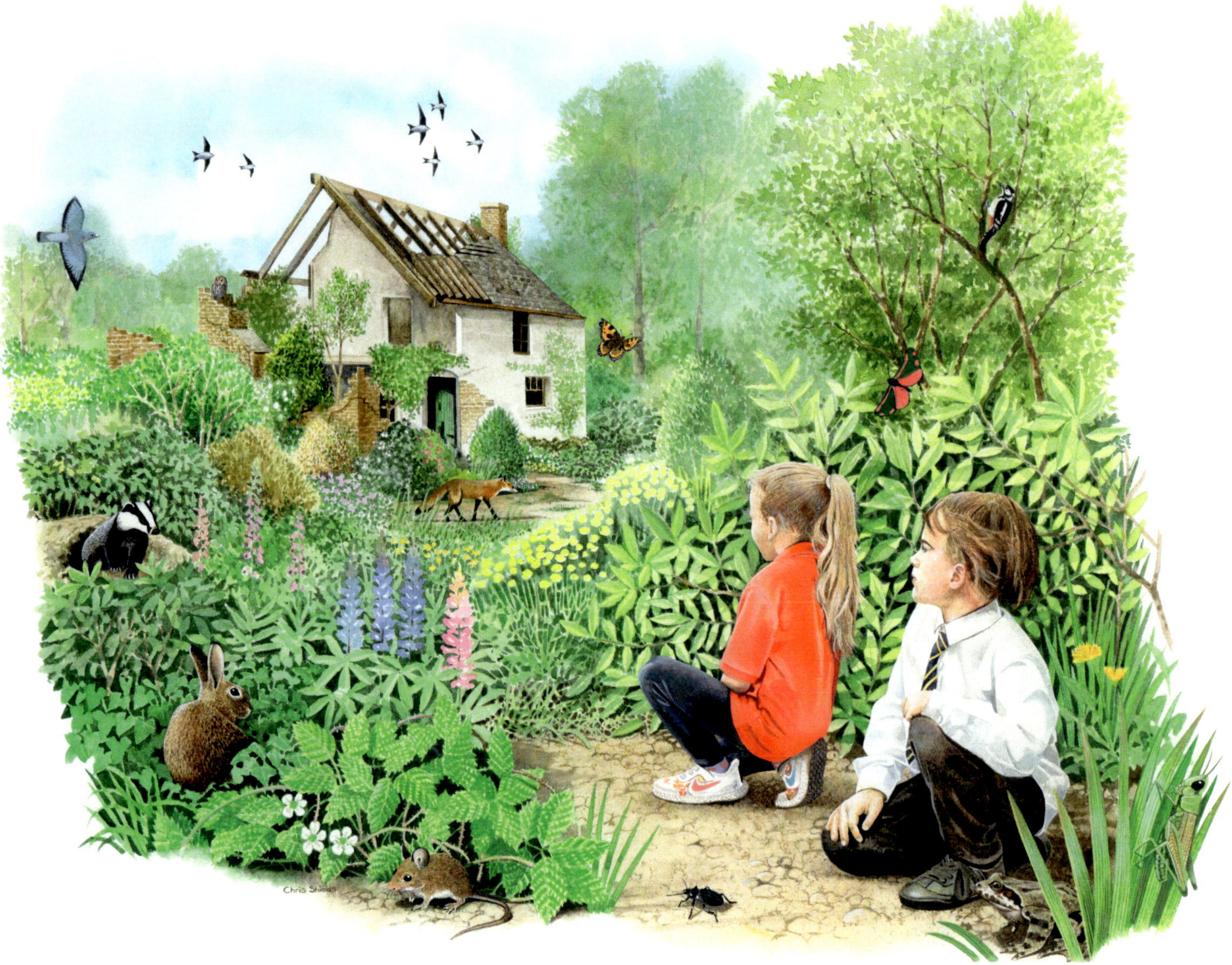
Chris Shields

Mo the small brown bat snuggled down sleepily. It was dawn and she had returned to her roost from a busy night hunting insects. Her tummy was full of mosquitoes, moths and midges.

Mo and her friends roosted inside the chimney of an old tumbledown cottage on the edge of a village.

It was the perfect bat hideout, warm and sheltered, with lots of nooks and crannies for Mo and her batty friends to snooze in during the daytime.

Mo is roosting with other female bats. In spring female bats get together somewhere warm and dry to have their babies. Male bats roost separately in buildings and trees

People couldn't live in the cottage anymore and wildlife had moved in. Long grasses rustled in the porch, wild honeysuckle curled around the stairs, willowherb and cow parsley jostled in the living room.

Spiders spun webs in the cupboards and beetles scurried along the cracks between the tiles in the bathroom.

A family of foxes lived under the kitchen sink.

Badgers had dug themselves a sett in the old vegetable patch at the bottom of the overgrown garden.

The village children thought the cottage was haunted.

No-one disturbed the wildlife living there.

Until one day...

A huge yellow monster turned up in the village.

It made the ground shake and was very noisy. Mo and her friends woke up, trembling with fear.

The monster trundled towards the cottage, its massive claw held menacingly above its head. Straight through the cottage roof and walls went the claw, raking out the floors and ceilings, ripping down the chimney.

Higgledy-piggledy out the bats flew.

When the dust settled all that was left of the cottage was a pile of rubble, bricks and broken wood.

Flying up into the sky, Mo felt sad and lost. Where would she and her friends live now?

Old buildings are sometimes knocked down to make way for new houses or because they are unsafe. Where a building is very old or special it is protected by law

Down the lane from the old cottage, in the middle of the village, stood a church. It was made of soft yellow sandstone and was tall and handsome with coloured glass windows and a grey roof. It was over 800 years old and was full of precious and beautiful things.

Every day Bob Chandler visited. He was the churchwarden and his job was to look after the church and keep it clean and safe.

Today he swept the floors and tidied the hymn books. He dusted the pews and polished the new brass candlesticks to keep them bright and shiny.

It was usually very peaceful while he cleaned, but today he heard a sudden loud crashing and splintering noise in the distance.

He went to the church door and looked out, squinting in the bright sunshine. At the far end of the lane, right at the edge of the village, he saw a huge cloud of dust.

"I bet that's the old cottage being knocked down to make way for new houses," he sighed before returning to his dusting and polishing.

Mo and her friends flew around frantically, looking for shelter. They needed to find a new home. They didn't like being outside in the daytime when predators like sparrowhawks and crows might be about, waiting to snatch a plump tasty little bat out of the air.

Suddenly Mo saw a big stone building up ahead.

It didn't have a chimney like the tumbledown cottage but it did have a clock tower, and some of its windows were brightly coloured.

Like a rainbow, Mo thought.

The stone building had a peaceful and cared for feel to it, with lots of nooks and crannies. Just the sort of place bats like to roost in.

"Over here!" Mo squeaked to her friends.

Many bat roosting sites, such as ancient trees and buildings like the cottage, have disappeared. Churches are often the only places left for bats to roost in

The bats circled round the building, trying to find a way in.

Mo spotted a small gap in the roof. She poked her head through it and then crawled carefully inside. She found herself in a dark space under the roof tiles. A spider was busily spinning a web in one corner.

"In here," she called to her friends. In they all scrambled, cuddling together for comfort and warmth.

Mo was happy. She had found a new place to call home.

Mo decided to explore. The roof space was dusty and dim, but a soft light shone from some gaps. Curious, Mo poked her head through one of these.

She gasped. It was the most beautiful place she had ever seen. Light flickered from candles on a wide table at one end. There were lots of long wooden seats and colourful cushions on the floor.

Mo went to take a closer look. Like most bats she was very nosy. As she dropped out of the roof space, she unfurled her wings and flittered into the cool interior.

Over her head was a high beamed ceiling that reminded Mo of tree branches. It made her feel safe. She swooped about with her mouth wide open shouting her special bat shout.

As well as being nosy, bats are extremely noisy, but humans can't hear them because the sound is too high pitched for our ears. The sound wave from their shouts bounces off objects, making an echo. By listening to these echoes, bats create a sound picture of what is around them. This is called echolocation

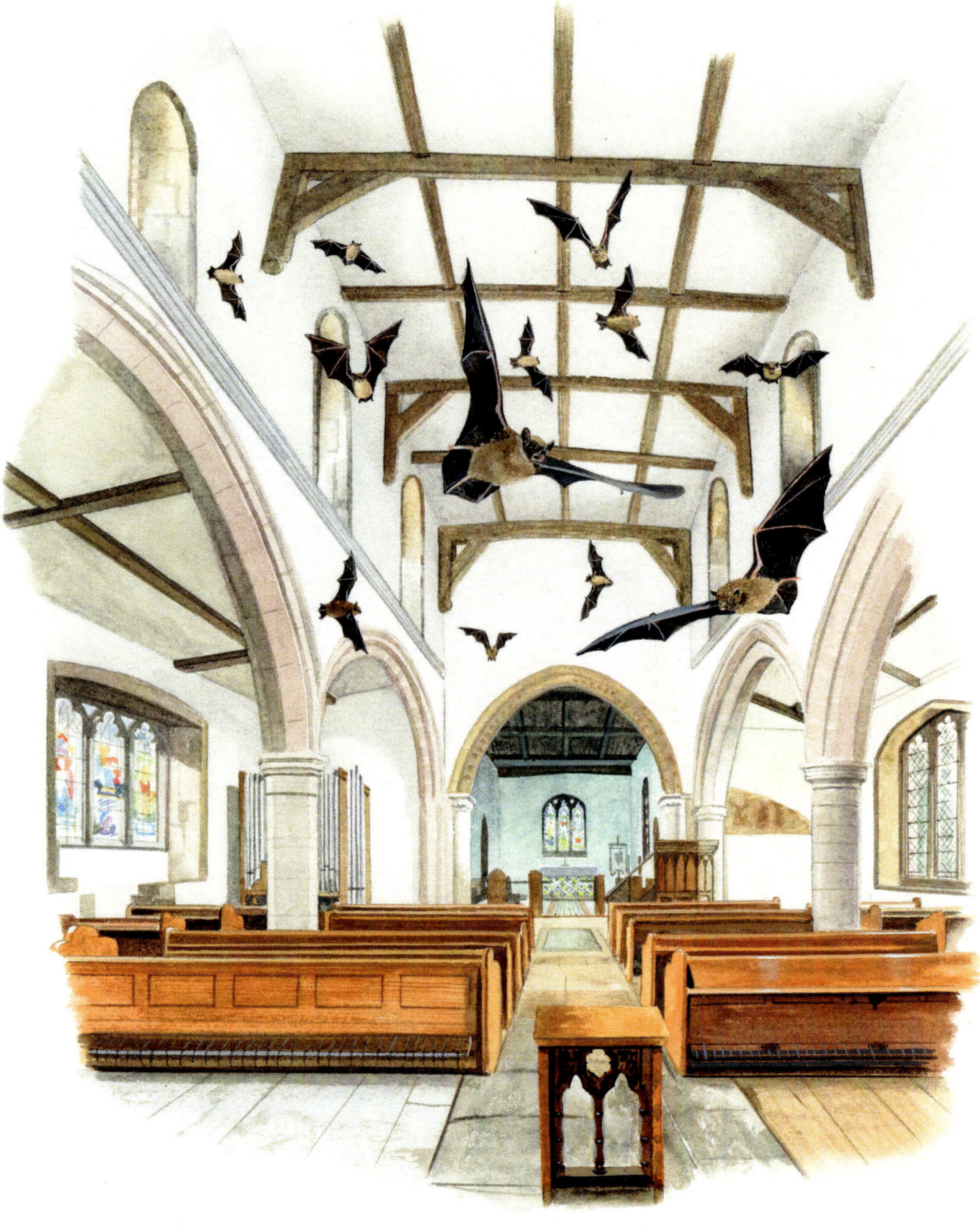

That evening, before heading out to catch their breakfast, Mo and her friends had a party inside the church, swooping and chasing, chattering and gossiping, and generally having the time of their lives.

The next morning, when Bob went in to sweep and dust and polish, he saw lots of tiny black specks and dark wet patches all over the floor, pews and window ledges.

"Oh dear," he said. "That looks like mouse poo and wee!"

He bent down to peer at the specks. They were dry and crumbly.

"This isn't mouse poo," he cried. "This is bat poo. I bet the bats were in that old cottage and now they've moved into the church!"

Poor Bob had a lot of sweeping and mopping up to do that morning.

Bats eat a lot of insects and so they produce a lot of poo! Unlike mouse poo, bat poo is dry and crumbly as it is made from the outer casings of all the insects they eat

The days turned into weeks and Mo and her friends settled happily into their new home.

Every evening, when it began to get dark, they would have a bat party inside the church before flying outside to hunt for insects.

Spring turned into summer. Now she felt safe and secure, Mo decided it was a good time to have a baby. Mo's friends had babies as well. Soon there were twice as many bats in the church as before!

Over the summer Mo's baby grew bigger and stronger. She called him Milo.

At about six weeks old Milo began to fly around and catch insects all by himself.

Every day Bob went to the church and cleaned. Every day there was more mess. People were starting to complain about the smell and the bat poo. It was all getting too much.

"I am going to have to do something about this," said Bob. "I know, I'll call Jenny. She lives in the village and knows all about bats."

Jenny was an ecologist, a wildlife expert. Bats were her favourite animal.

"Well, you've definitely got bats!" she exclaimed as she walked into the church. "I'll come back at night to count them and see how many there are."

Later that evening she returned with a camera that could film the bats at night, and special detectors to hear the bat shouts. Then she and Bob waited for the bats to wake up.

Bats usually give birth to a single pup in the summer. Like us bats are mammals and bat pups feed on their mother's milk. Newborn pups are pink and hairless and about the size of a baked bean. They grow soft downy grey fur when they are a few days old

As it got dark the bats came pouring out of the church. Bob gasped in amazement, "I had no idea there were so many!"

"No wonder it's a struggle to keep the church clean," said Jenny.

"I like bats, but I wish they wouldn't make such a mess inside the church. Is there anything we can do?" Bob asked.

"There must be," she replied. "Let me have a think."

By autumn the bats were ready to leave their church roost. They needed to eat a lot of insects and get nice and fat before finding somewhere quiet to sleep through the winter.

Milo went off into the forest with some of the other young bats to chase insects and have fun.

"Bye Milo," shouted Mo. "Have a good life son," she yelled after him at the top of her voice.

But Milo flew off without so much as a backward glance. He had his own life to lead, his own friends to make, his own flight path to follow.

Mo felt a little sad … but not for long. She knew that Milo had to learn to look after himself.

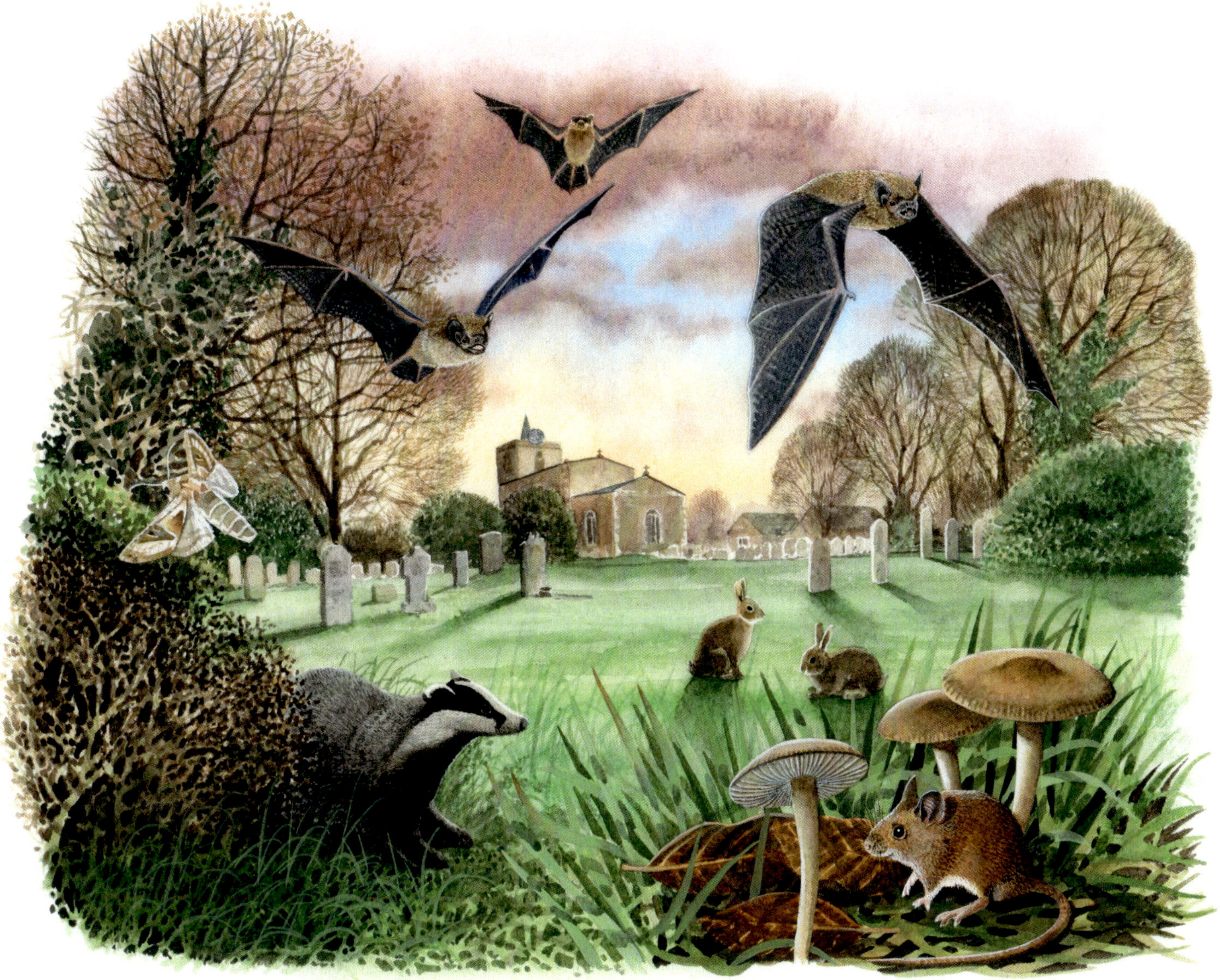

Winter came...

As the weather gets colder there are fewer insects to eat so bats find a cool place to spend the winter. Their heart rate and breathing becomes very slow and their body temperature falls as well. This deep sleep is called hibernation

While Mo and her batty friends spent the winter hibernating, people were very busy at the church.

Bob called Corinne. Corinne was a church architect who understood church buildings and how special they are.

While Bob swept and polished, Jenny and Corinne climbed up a ladder and peered into the roof space, taking measurements and making sketches. They chatted as they worked.

Together they all drew up a plan and called some builders.

The builders got to work. They made some special bat shelters for the bats in the roof space and filled the gaps to stop the bats getting inside the church. When they finished they even hoovered up all the dust!

As the days grew longer and warmer, bright green shoots pushed up out of the ground, spring flowers unfurled, birds trilled and chirruped, and insects busily buzzed, scuttled and fluttered.

Mo opened her eyes. She shivered to get warm, stretched her wings and yawned loudly, showing her sharp little teeth. Spring had sprung!

Out she sped into the cool evening air, over the woods and rivers, the fields and hedgerows, and the narrow country lanes.

She was very hungry after her long winter sleep. She spent the night foraging for insects until her little tummy was completely full. As the sun came up she started looking for somewhere to roost.

Ahead she saw the beautiful stone building that had sheltered her and her friends so many months before.

Mo was very happy to find her summer home still standing.

Mo found the gap in the roof and wriggled through. What a difference!

The dusty roof space was now clean. The holes to the inside of the church had been filled, and there were lots of new nooks and crannies, perfect for bats to snuggle up in.

"Hey girls," she yelled to her friends. "Check out the new nursery!"

That evening the whole village gathered in the churchyard to watch the bats. Jenny explained how to use the bat detectors to hear the bats' special shout.

Bob showed everyone around the nice clean church, with its rainbow windows, polished pews and sparkling candlesticks.

"It's all worked out brilliantly," he told them. "The bats have somewhere to live, and I am not being driven batty cleaning up bat poo!"

As the sun set, Mo and her friends had their party in the churchyard, swooping and chasing, chattering and gossiping, and generally having the time of their lives.

The End

With thanks to everyone who helps care for bats and churches

Discover More About Bats In Churches

HOW TRUE IS MO'S STORY?

Mo's story is based on the real life story of the bats in a church near Oakham in Rutland.

WHAT SORT OF BAT IS MO?

Mo is a Soprano Pipistrelle, the smallest type of bat found in Britain. Soprano Pipistrelles have a wingspan of about 20cm and are about the weight of a 20p coin. Like many bat species, adult female Soprano Pipistrelles spend the summer in maternity colonies. They usually give birth in June to a single pup, but can occasionally have twins.

DO BATS LIKE MO REALLY PARTY?

Yes! Soprano Pipistrelles hang out in groups called colonies. They often fly around together outside their roosts at dusk and dawn.

DO BATS LIKE TO LIVE IN CHURCHES?

They certainly do! Old churches have lots of space and are full of nooks and crannies for bats to roost in. They're like a man-made forest and a perfect place for bats to live. At least half of the UK's 17 breeding species of bats have been found in churches.

WHY DO BATS NEED TO BE PROTECTED?

There are far fewer bats in the UK now than there were 100 years ago. There are fewer places for bats to live, and their homes have been destroyed through development and building works. More roads and street lighting make it harder for bats to find food. Because of this, bats are legally protected and it is a crime to harm them or damage their roosts.

WHY DO CHURCHES NEED TO BE PROTECTED?

Churches are places of worship and beautiful, historic buildings that tell the story of our past. Many of our churches are hundreds of years old and are full of fascinating treasures such as wall paintings, statues, brasses and metalwork, wood and stone carvings, and stained glass.

Around the country thousands of people like Bob care for churches. By protecting churches we help keep them safe for future generations to cherish.

WHAT PROBLEMS CAN BATS CAUSE IN CHURCHES?

Just like in the story, bats can make a lot of mess when they roost and fly inside church buildings. Bats' poo and wee can stain and damage wood, stone and metal, and make a lot of extra work for those who look after the church.

The mess can mean that people don't want to go inside the church any more. In a few cases the situation can get so bad the church has to close.

HOW CAN YOU HELP?

If you'd like to find out more about bats you can see if there is a local Bat Group you can join.

Your local Wildlife Trust, Natural History Society or Mammal Group might also run bat events. You can contact your local church and see if they'd like any help, for example if they're running any events or raising money to help look after the church.

There are lots of fun bat and church activities on the Bats In Churches website, including how to look for signs of bats in your local church.

batsinchurches.org.uk

🐦 @BatsinChurches   ❑ BatsInChurchesProject

About the Bats In Churches Project

The Bats In Churches Project was formed as a unique partnership between Natural England, Church of England, Bat Conservation Trust, The Churches Conservation Trust and Historic England. Funded by the National Lottery Heritage Fund the project ran from 2019 to 2023.

The project has worked with churches, bat ecologists, church architects, heritage experts and bat groups to find long term, practical solutions to help churches coexist with their bats. These included making new bat roosts, building voids and flight spaces, creating bat free areas inside the church, putting up bat boxes in churchyards, and installing protection for organs, monuments and memorials. Where bats or their roosts were likely to be disturbed, work was usually carried out under the new Bats In Churches Class Licence developed by Natural England specifically for the Bats In Churches Project.

The project organised cleaning workshops and trained volunteers to support and advise churches with bats, and to survey churches for bats.

It also ran a variety of engagement events including church bat walks, heritage talks and events, online talks and lectures, and school workshops.

About the Illustrator

Chris Shields, award-winning artist and wildlife illustrator, is regarded as one of the world's leading natural history illustrators. He is a keen naturalist and has produced in excess of 30,000 wildlife illustrations in over 300 books, and created work for organisations such as the RSPB, The Wildlife Trusts, Friends of the Earth, The Oregon State History Museum USA, BBC Wildlife Magazine and The Field Studies Council.

About the Authors

Rose and Diana have worked on the Bats In Churches Project since its start in 2019.

Diana has been working with communities, heritage and wildlife for over 15 years. Her work has included bird of prey reintroduction, managing visitors at Scottish seabird reserves for the RSPB and a historic parkland restoration project in Aberdeenshire. She worked for the Bats In Churches project across East England.

Rose worked with churches with bats in the North and Midlands. She has an abiding interest in both historic churches and bats, and is a member of Derbyshire Bat Group. She previously worked as an environmental educator for the Peak District National Park Authority and Derbyshire Wildlife Trust.